I0755895

INTO THE NIGHT THAT FLIES SO FAST

First published in 2024 by
The Dedalus Press
13 Moyclare Road
Baldoyle
Dublin D13 K1C2
Ireland

www.dedaluspress.com

ISBN 978-1-915629-17-3 (paperback)
ISBN 978-1-915629-16-6 (hardback)

Dedalus Press titles are available in Ireland
from Argosy Books (www.argosybooks.ie) and in the UK
from Inpress Books (www.inpressbooks.co.uk)

Cover image: 'Mirror' by Colin Murphy,
Oil on wood panel.
By permission of the artist.
https://colinmurphyart.com

The Dedalus Press receives financial assistance from
The Arts Council / An Chomhairle Ealaíon.

INTO THE NIGHT THAT FLIES SO FAST

MILENA WILLIAMSON

DEDALUS PRESS

Contents

INTERVAL

ACT THREE

for Bridget Cleary, 1869 (?) – 15 March, 1895

A young woman has met her death under circumstances which remind us of the lines:

> 'Pleading like angels, trumpet-tongued,
> Against the deep damnation of her taking off.'

—Justice William O'Brien

I will not allow a question as to where fairies are supposed to be. They may be supposed to be in this courthouse. We are not here acting a play, but to inquire into matters of fact.

—Justice William O'Brien

ACT ONE

Lawful

[Awake BRIDGET BOLAND, Bridget's mother, who is dead]

Three young boys
and two policemen
disturb the earth
beside me
burying the burnt knot
of her body
under the cover
of night.
She smells of soot
sun-dried sheets
chicken soup
and stirabout.
The boy with the lamp
reads a prayer
and in the tremulous glow
of guesswork
he makes the story
a little kinder.
I pour my graces
upon my daughter.
My spell is lawful—
tell me, mine own.

Early one morning, my partner and I pack our weekend bags. The cherry tree outside our flat is bursting with pink blossoms. This time next year, it will be toppled by an unexpected cold snap, its snow-covered flowers cascading across the driveway. But today it is still in bloom. *Ready?* my partner E asks. I nod, double-checking my backpack: water bottle, walking shoes, notebook, maps. In the car, I start the GPS and find the road-trip playlist on my phone. I have a list of places I want to visit in County Tipperary: a graveyard, a church, a house. The remnants of what happened one cold spring night in 1895. In our hybrid rental car, we are outfitted for the future as we drive into the past. The hours pass easily. E listens to me worry about my writing again. I listen to him talk about running again. Having met during the first few months of the pandemic, we are comfortable in each other's company. At the end of the journey, we take a wrong turn. We drive round and round on rural roads, looking for the farm lane that leads to our Airbnb. Eventually we stop in Rathgormack. In the local shop, we breathe in the sweet floury smell of fresh soda bread, scones, apple tarts and cinnamon rolls. I pass by the display of Bibles and choose a homemade jam instead. E is on the phone with the Airbnb host. The woman behind the counter looks to be about my age. She is wearing a long skirt, cardigan and apron despite the warm weather. *Where are you from?* she asks. *We drove down from Belfast today,* I say, *but I'm from Pennsylvania.* She explains that she has always wanted to visit Pennsylvania and meet more Amish-Mennonite people. *I didn't know there was an Amish community in Ireland,* I say. *There was someone else from Pennsylvania in the shop yesterday,* she replies.

No.

Chief Secretary's Office, Ireland.

POLICE & CRIME DIVISION (ORDINARY.) 6694

SUBJECT.	MINUTE.
Co Tipperary Murder of Bridget Cleary. – Report from Crown Solicitor. He hopes to have Magisterial investigation closed today (5.4.95)	Chief Secretary, WHK 5.4.95 [illegible] 6.4.95 ✓ [illegible] 8.4.95

The Bower

[Enter BRIDGET CLEARY]

I rise with the rain and toss potato skins to the dog.
The cat claws her way onto my shoulder.

The hens lay eggs, dawn's pearly punctuation.
If a hare sucked from the cows last night, so be it.

A fox weaves through the furze, returning to her cubs
with a rat between her jaws, a pendulum of love.

There are many goodly creatures here!
Yet every man's whistle hangs upon the chain.

Down the low road and up the hill, through the fields
and into the grove, I wander weeping over flowers.

Any broken branch could form a cradle—
my husband carves emptiness into barrels.

Water pools in my boots. My lips shed like lace.
I shiver and disremember the hour of my return.

The Hollow Ground

[Enter DISTRICT INSPECTOR WANSBROUGH, who searches for Bridget]

The key rasps in the lock
and I walk where she walked.
In the bedroom, I collect the saucepan
and inspect the shovel, spade and can.

The spade is new and the handle is stained,
held by someone with an oily hand.
I get a whiff of paraffin oil.
The shovel has traces of marshy soil

like that of the earth where yesterday,
bending low, I uncovered her body—
I held my ear to the hollow ground
then followed the bog down and down.

Did the family wash this filthy witness
from their hands? Did they wash
at all after digging down, brainsickly
after seeing the gilded face of their lady.

Tender

[Enter JOHANNA BURKE, Bridget's cousin, who is a mother of six children dead and alive]

Lifting her head
I coax her
to have a sup

of something,
beestings to tempt her
back on her feet.

Once we lay
on our bellies
and drank from the stream.

Once she was
my bridesmaid
gossiping by my side.

I will not touch
a private penny
for my milk.

She must not
rub my shilling
under her bedding.

Let the fire
do its work
to warm her.

I am big-bellied again
and again I summon
the wanton wind.

My own wee Bridget
arrived early, wasting away
or fairy-stricken.

She did not last.
How tender it was
to love the babe.

The fold stands empty
in the drowned field,
crows are fattened

with ailing flock
and my womb is rich
with what is owed.

We are spending the weekend in a converted outhouse on a farm near Carrick-on-Suir. There is fresh milk in a pitcher on the windowsill and fairy lights in the rafters. An ash tree once grew in the bedroom. In the corner by the stove, there is a small dining table. The farmer apologises for it, wiping his face with the back of his hand. The table is the perfect size for my partner and me to sit with our knees touching, which is how we like to have our meals. E asks the man how the farm is doing. *Okay, but this morning a calf was born out of season. Nature can amaze and disappoint us.* The two of them launch into a conversation about milking and the old-fashioned machines versus the new robotic ones that can be synced to your smartphone. *Are you here for business or pleasure?* the farmer asks. I try to explain that I am writing about a woman who lived nearby at the turn of the last century. Picking at the hem of my shirt, I'm unsure whether to mention the unusual circumstances of her death. Bridget Cleary's family may have believed that she had been abducted and replaced with a fairy. The man scratches the dried mud on his arm and glances out the window. I can feel my cheeks getting hot. I'm self-conscious about my accent here. I am another foreigner asking questions even after all this time. Our host reminds us to leave the keys in the door when we go. An acquaintance who lives in Clonmel told me, *don't trust a word the locals say, or maybe don't say anything about what you're up to.* Across the farmyard, the milking shed is quiet.

Every Inch of Woman in the World

[Enter PATRICK KENNEDY, Bridget's cousin, who pins her to the bed]

She melted into air.
We carried the body up the hill
and buried her with care.
She melted into air,
every inch of her.
It makes me ill,
how she melted into air
and we walked down the hill.

There's Some Wonder in This Handkerchief

[Enter BADGER, Bridget's dog, who barks at journalists]

I follow the scent
from her feathered hat
hanging on a nail
to a blue handkerchief
crumpled on the floor—
there's magic in the web of it,
this last remembrance
from her husband
that my lady reserves
evermore about her.
I follow the scent
to one gold earring
glinting in the ashes
and to her husband
who is scraping off the juice
of some poor creature.
I follow the scent to her body.
She lies in the outhouse
and it masks her smell.
The peelers guard her
and I guard the outhouse
like the gates of hell.
I lie in the dung
and there is not a woman
who comes up the road
who could be her.

A Butter-Woman

[Enter WILLIAM SIMPSON, Bridget's neighbour, who possesses the keys to the Cleary's house]

She often brought me eggs, a bit of banter
and nothing more. A good neighbour,
she calmed the cows and sang their milk to butter.

Certain women can charm the butter,
this we know, we know for sure.
Rub the creature with your hand or boot or

bundle a blue stone in a petticoat for better
luck and by morning her pearly udders
will be ample, the stream of milk much brighter.

City-folk who think they know better
than fairy-stories come knocking on my door.
They ask questions and offer gifts to butter

me up, but my neighbour was never a bother.
Strange to think I won't see her anymore,
neither her nor her pup Badger.

She crossed my fields, empty but for
the cows who lowed for more.
It's true, my tongue loved a butter-
woman's mouth, an egg out of a cloister.

The Time of Night

[Enter DOTEY, Bridget's cat, who watches everyone]

Now it is the time of night
when I prowl into the rath.
All is amplified: the smell of earth,
the rustle of mice, food and drink,
battles and songs, ancient rites,
everything that came before—
it's raining. My fur is wet.
I skulk home and curl myself
into a warm knot beside my mistress.

Cloneen is a rural village bookended by the GAA club and the church. My partner and I sit on the wall in front of the GAA club and unwrap our packed lunch. A ginger cat appears. E never pets cats he doesn't know, but I extend my hand. Maybe it is me or maybe it is the wafer-thin smoked ham on my sandwich, but the cat jumps onto my lap. She purrs and looks at me expectantly. I feed her a bit of meat. My stomach gurgles. Maybe I have travelled so far to feel exactly this. After lunch, we walk up the quiet main road to the Church of the Visitation. I begin my search for Bridget at the end of her life, where she was buried after her body was discovered. In the cemetery, two men are up to their waists in a fresh grave. They could be the gravediggers who bury Ophelia, arguing over whether she deserves a Christian burial. I murmur hello. They look up from their work and nod. E studies the platitudes on new headstones and suggests going row by row. I drift away from him, towards crumbling graves and uncut grass. He doesn't know Bridget is buried beside a wall, on the border between sacred and unholy ground. The policemen lifted her body into the churchyard from the other side. Only rocks mark her grave. Bridget is buried next to her mother, who also has no headstone. When my partner finds me, I am sitting in the grass. I am sitting beside the woman in my head.

Honey Breath

[Enter MARY KENNEDY, Bridget's widowed aunt, who cares for Bridget during her illness]

Who is this? My niece flies away so fast.
She raves of planets and a pain in her head.
For her mother's sake, I will not part with her.
To bring her back, I kill a chicken, pluck it clean
and boil fat with milk. To bring her back,
the men try herbs, medicine or moonshine.
She must swallow it. I wind the clock and stir the cinders.
If she had her mother, she would not be this way.

When she opens a coffee tin full of banknotes,
the men breathe honey beside her bed.
Tonight she will ride a white horse to the future.
If I do dream, all her wealth would wake me
and if she is dreaming, I would follow her
into the night that flies so fast.

Sweeter Creature

[Enter MICHAEL CLEARY, Bridget's husband, who is sleepless after ten days and nights]

I threw no paraffin oil on my wife, nor neither
was there oil in the house, only what she herself
poured from a bottle into a lamp that was lighting.

I did not place her on the fire.
The world hath not a sweeter creature
and she was too fine to be my wife.

We cut her from the sweet creature
she rode in the dark. She cried, unpin me
and death's unnatural that kills for loving.

One of her legs was shorter than the other,
said the man who took her measure,
whose own limp was just a farmyard fracture.

One of her legs was longer than the other,
said the man who measured her in bed.
When a changeling walks, she skips.

I have no wife. It was the very error of the moon—
she came more nearer earth than she was wont
and made men mad.

An Old Tale

[Re-enter BRIDGET CLEARY]

Always faithful
the sparrows return.

The pair sculpts a nest
under the eaves

and in the darkness
of the outhouse

I line my underwear
with clean rags.

That which is true
is like an old tale—

there was a woman
who dwelt by a mountain.

I kneel and pray
for my flesh and blood.

The Understudy

[I sit backstage, dressed for the part I do not play: two petticoats, a flannel dress, a cashmere jacket and a shawl. I sweat beneath my stockings and leave my stays unlaced. Do you want help getting out of your costume later, asks the stagehand. I draw a circle around myself with salt. I have heard the rumours about why I did not get the role: I am allergic to dogs, I failed to cast a spell in my audition, I identify too well with the character. I mouth the actress's lines to charm her tongue, rub the burn mark on my dress and swallow four spoonfuls of medicine three times a day. An actor says, we have no such daughter, nor shall we ever see that face of hers again.]

ACT TWO

I Must Be Thy Lady

[Enter BRIDGET CLEARY]

After my mother took like a trembling,
some called me queer. I was stricken

by books or hens or needle and thread,
machines of moonlit revels.

My husband begs for a little boy.
We could rear him up, he says,

holding me above the kitchen hearth.
What are the lines I learn by heart?

Give me a chance, I must be thy lady.
You are making an emergency of me.

My husband hums a nursery rhyme:
are you, are you, or are you a wife?

A dog howls at the offstage moon
and my mother appears in the doorway.

Thrice

[Enter JAMES KENNEDY, Bridget's cousin, who holds her by the hand]
[Enter WILLIAM KENNEDY, Bridget's cousin, who holds her by the feet]
[Enter MICHAEL KENNEDY, Bridget's cousin, who faints]

We carried her from the bed to the fire.
Thrice we asked her for her name
and she refused to answer.
We held her above the fire
and did not burn her.
She's a changeling or the same.
We carried her back to bed after the fire.
Thrice we begged her for her name.

Some Natural Notes About Her Body

[Enter DR. CREAN, who drinks on the job]
[Enter DR. HEFFERNAN, who is married with children]

We have carried out our examination:
her cheeks were flushed, discoloured
perhaps by a person holding the neck.

We removed her scalp and discovered
the vessels of the brain were congested
as were the lungs. The spleen was ruptured.

We found no great marks of violence.
Organs protruded from burned apertures.
The bones of the spine were exposed.

We judged her stomach to be healthy.
She suffered from nervous excitement
but the remains are well nourished.

We hereby conclude: the right hand
was contracted and the fingers charred.
The tongue was lacerated as if she tried to talk.

At the graveside, my partner asks, *What was Bridget's favourite colour?* This is one of many impossible questions. *Blue, I guess.* I explain to him that she was wearing a lot of blue when she was burned to death. We wander into the middle of the graveyard and under an archway. A small plaque informs us that during a tidy-up of the graveyard a thirteenth-century medieval grave slab was discovered. We find the remains of the medieval church. Ivy clings to the broken walls and wildflowers of almost every colour burst from the rubble. Red valerian, love-in-a-mist, marigolds, poppies, cow parsley and cornflowers. They are thriving in the fertile ground. I pick a few flowers and we return to Bridget's grave. E says a prayer, one Bridget would have known: *Eternal rest grant unto them, O Lord…* I balance a pebble on top of her rough gravestone. Bridget almost certainly would not have known this Jewish tradition, but it's one small thing I can offer. On the other side of the wall, there's a yellow bulldozer and the shell of a new house. We pass the gravediggers again as we leave, and I tell E to ask them about the graveyard. I'm wary of asking men questions while they are holding shovels or any other heavy implement. E says hello and they stop digging. He asks them about the old unmarked graves. *Stones were enough to remember,* they say, *at a time not long ago when everyone knew everyone in the village.* E thanks them for their help, and they ask him if he is from the North. *I'm a County Down man,* he replies. They offer him the name of a local historian and tell us we will find him in the shop today but not tomorrow. They are digging this grave for his aunt.

The Raven and the Lark

[Enter PATRICK BOLAND, Bridget's father, who is losing his sight]

When my wife began to wither
our daughter tended to her.
Together they made an alphabet.

Bridget's milk turned to marble,
the butter turned and I had no one
in the world to turn to. It was not me

did ever lay a finger on her.
The body was of middle height
with regular features and blue eyes.

My daughter was a woman,
a rich ornament of what I meant.
A raven does not hatch a lark

so she will come home to me.
Bridgie will come back like a bird,
singing sweet tidings of the sun's uprise.

Beyond My Practice

[Enter DENIS GANEY, the fairy-doctor,
who prescribes a herbal remedy for Bridget]

Away over the mountain, there is a rumour
she is troubled with thick coming fancies.
Eyes closed, I crawl through the garden

searching for a green that knows itself,
a leaf to light her eyes and then some—
a little something to soften her nights.

The peelers drag me over my threshold,
saying I am an accessory before the fact
and I never set foot in her house.

Did any man see me? Did he say I assisted
in doing away with the sickly woman?
Her disease was beyond my practice.

Imprisoned, I grow thinner until
I escape my cell through the keyhole.
I have never needed to heal a woman twice.

Withered and Wild

[Enter FATHER RYAN, who administers the last rites to Bridget]

When I next saw her husband
he was on his knees in the chapel,
scrubbing his hands.

He wanted to go to confession
but he was not in a fit state
to receive the sacrament.

If I had heard of witchcraft
I would never have returned
or said Mass in that house.

Did she spit out the sacrament?
I would not like to swear it untrue
but I do not think it is true.

She seemed to understand me.
She was so withered and wild
and looked not of the earth.

The Candle and the Charmed Pot

[Enter WILLIAM AHEARNE, Bridget's neighbour, who is a boy of sixteen]

I held the candle aloft.
The men circled round her bed.
Milk boiled in the charmed pot.
I held the candle aloft
so the men could use the light.
Milk bubbled and the candle burned.
I held the candle aloft.
The men circled round her bed.

On the narrow country road, my partner and I are forced into the hedge as tractors pass. *You should be wearing a high-vis,* a farmer calls out, *self-preservation is a virtue. Next time,* I reply. This is the last walk Bridget ever did, heading up the hill and returning home to Ballyvadlea with flushed cheeks. This was the last time she was ever outside. E and I don't linger at her house, which has been renovated. I explain how the chimneys in each gable mark the original structure and what might have happened at the hearth. A family of teddies looks out from an upstairs window. A Bród flag hangs in a downstairs window. E tells me the make and model of the cars in the driveway, but I have turned away from the present towards the green hills of Slievenamon, the mountain of the women. It has taken years of research and hours of driving to get here, but after a few minutes, E and I leave. On the main road back to Cloneen, we meet a man walking his dog. The dog wags his tail, so I ask the man if there are any nearby ring forts, the ones that some people associate with fairies. He confirms my research that they are hard to find and are often situated on private land. *Why take your chances,* he says, *most farmers work around them and eventually the ring forts become overgrown.* 'Fairy' is a pothole in his tongue.

Done Quickly

[Enter JACK DUNNE, Bridget's father's cousin, a storyteller who walks with a limp]

There was no night of my life
I never heard the fairies hurling.
They called me to the rath
but my aching leg was crooked.

I never heard the fairies calling
until she called me to her bedside.
My aching leg was crooked
and she was nothing but herself.

At the woman's bedside
I had to jump the life to come.
She was nothing of herself,
the whole matter and copy.

With all my life, I jumped upon her
wielding fire to make her answer
whether she was matter or copy.
A hot poker could bring her back.

If there is fire in her answer
then well it were done quickly.
A hot poker might bring her back
from whence the fairies call her.

The Iron Tongue

[Enter MARY KENNEDY, Bridget's widowed aunt, who works for lodgings on Justice O'Brien's property]

It was late in the night, long after
the iron tongue of midnight had tolled twelve,
when her husband took out holy water.
He held it to her lips. She drank it down.
She rose and dressed and sat by the fire.
I made bread and jam and tea for everyone.
I lay in her bed and when I awoke she was
wearing only a chemise. She was ablaze.

I told the cursed story to the judge,
naming all the actors who orbited the girl.
I told our cursed story in the courthouse
and someone set fire to my cottage.
The thatch burned. The charred earth
was a stage where no one set foot again.

Haunting

[Enter MICHAEL CLEARY, who is Convict 6866]

I have been to and from
the roof of the carpenter's shop
dozens of times and always
the same way I went this morning
but on coming down today
my foot slipped and I fell.
She haunts me everywhere
the fairies haunt the ground.

We are the only ones in the Church of the Immaculate Conception in Drangan. There are several pictures of Pope Francis, and yellow caution tape cordons off every second pew. I wander around looking for the confession booth even though Bridget's husband spoke to the priests in the chapel yard. Bridget's husband walked here after she died. He might have wanted to confess. He might have believed the priests could bring her back from the fairies. I step onto the altar. *Don't do that,* says my partner, *you can't stand there.* I look down at the salmon-coloured carpet. *It's just the floor,* I say, but I step down anyway. E likes the silence in the chapel, but I prefer the silence in nature: the stream trickling, the wind in the leaves and the squeak of a rusty gate. A local story recalls how Bridget's dog attacked a priest as he rode by on his horse. When the priest kicked the dog, Bridget threw boiling water at him. He cursed her with death by fire. I take E's hand and lead him out of the church. By the exit, I spot the grave of the parish priest who first heard the story of Bridget's murder. Across the street, we study the shrine in honour of the Blessed Virgin. A woman steps out of the house next to the shrine. She looks at us and begins to sweep the pavement, moving closer and closer to the sacred spot, until finally she sweeps us off the path.

Ill Met by Moonlight

[Re-enter BRIDGET CLEARY]

Women, you will know the man
by the garments he has on.

While he walks to Fethard to fetch a herb,
women, skip hence and find me a flower

to charm his sight and make him madly
dote upon me or the next live creature.

He makes me the breathless housewife
by never giving me a drop of milk.

In this mazed world he tries to burn me
and it will be nothing by and by.

Here comes my husband.
We are ill met by moonlight.

I will never let the stains out of his clothes,
weeds wide enough to wrap a fairy in.

The Chorus

[I am wiping lipstick from my teeth when the door opens. Three women enter from another era, talking wildly. How could someone believe her lace thong was evidence. In the theatre of the bathroom, I roll a cigarette. Tell me about it, I say, the sergeant found my nightdress when he climbed through my window. He picked the lock and wrote it all down: such pictures, the adornment of my bed and the contents of the story, what I had been reading late. He stole my nightdress and used it as proof in court. Proof of what exactly, echo the chorus of women and I cannot remember, as if I were asleep when it happened. The women touch my arm, maybe a motherly touch.]

INTERVAL

How to Be Well

Before I move to Belfast, I have mono.
My god-daughter calls it moan-a
and cries when she cannot kiss me.
She sends me a card with a drawing
of a fairy and a note: *I hope you fell better.*

Before I have mono, I have pneumonia.
Alone in the emergency room,
I breathe sour air from a tube.
The doctor mispronounces my name
and slides the IV into my writing hand.

Before I have pneumonia, I get my period.
I fold toilet paper into my underwear.
I walk to school and it falls out:
a pishogue on the sidewalk
and a curse upon whoever owns the land.

Before I get my period, I have an MRI.
Doctors feel a lump in my stomach.
My father holds me to his chest
and ferries me into the machine.
The lump disappears before it is found.

Before I have an MRI, I am born.
The doctor's car battery has frozen.
My mother refuses the epidural
and I arrive before he does.
The nurse says I am beautiful.

Stranger

Walking farther than I have been before brings me to Tomb Street.
I'm a stone's throw away from Royal Mail, but I don't know where

and it's early days in Belfast and I've not got mail from anyone.
It's as good a street as any for learning how to look left and listen—

how's tricks catch yerself on aye meet yous at the back of Boots
I'll run ye over sure I almost lost the run of myself lookin at him.

I stand there searching for something déjà vu.
To feel like I have been before in a place I have never been

is all I can ask of this here city built on *wait until the green man*
shows opposite the north is next to let give way no ball games.

Feeling grows familiar as I peel a tangerine to smithereens.
I turn again into Tomb Street—*private gate keep clear*

queue here at any time on footway no persons beyond this point.
The inner ring does my head in as I follow it round and exit too early.

I call my father across the ocean and say *bout ye* are you there
ach sure ye know yerself can you hear me *right I'm away home.*

How to Make Latkes in Belfast

Use Yukon Gold or Idaho,
my mother writes in her letter.
You can find them anywhere but
maybe they have another name.
Review miracles. Don't measure.
Potatoes are surprisingly
acidic, so remember not
to grate your thumb. Pour the oil.
Drop the mixture into the pan.

On Our Night Out

He gets the steak and I get the chicken.
The waiter lights a candle.

We discuss our dreams:
in mine, moles invade my old house

and they nibble my neck.
His dream has teeth in all the wrong places

and he won't even hold my hand in public.
We chew the tough meat.

My first cat died in that house—
I buried Catty out front under the cherry tree.

His milky eye was still open: a piece of fat
the moon spat back. *It was a rental.*

My second cat died of shock
when I told him I fell

in love with a married man. Nobody
recorded the time of death. Tenderly

I fold my napkin
like a burning house.

On Our Last Night in Lancaster, Pennsylvania

I touch your knee. We leave the bar early,
but as we walk you realise your card
is gone. We loop back—
                                                  the construction paused
on the street, the closed Amish bakery
where the woman who opened the oven
wore a white bonnet, stiff as a dead dove,
where we ate pastries. We watch a car drive
past a horse-drawn carriage, moving over
into the opposite lane, a wide berth
since horses on the road spook easily.
Each driver looks up from his century
towards the other—
                                          At the bar, you hurry
inside while I wait by the door. I shoot
you a loving glance. It's still not too late.

The Outing

Did we travel on the north-south yellow
or east-west red? Apart or together
every day we played spot-the-most-tortured
security guard, saint or gargoyle.

Out of season, we tried a winter dish
of pomegranates, the one that translates
to beneath a snowy white carpet. It's
a carpet better shared with you. I wish

we had more souvenirs—an evening gown,
a monogrammed hairbrush, a nameless round
of hide and seek in the balcony room.
The blue canopy bed, an open tomb.

Let's buy walking sticks for when we are women
of another age, back home for teatime.

Love

adapted from the NHS page on pneumonia

It's more widespread in winter.
Symptoms can develop suddenly
or they may come on more slowly.
Your GP may listen to your chest
and check for crackling or rattling.
Are you breathing faster than usual?
Do you feel breathless even when resting?
Do you feel confused or disoriented?

Most cases can't be passed between people.
Mild cases can be treated at home.
It's usually safe for an infected person
to be around friends or family members.
It can affect anyone, but it's more serious
for the very young and the elderly.

The Hen Do

My first hen do begins by the sea
with cowgirl hats and a lunch
of oysters and champagne.
I order chips and sip slowly.
I have never eaten oysters—
my mother's rumoured allergy
and the meat too much like my tongue.

On the bus, there's wine and chocolates.
I take the sweets and keep the foil,
crinkling it between conversations.
There's line-dancing, Nash Bash,
trivia about the bride I cannot answer,
balloons we inflate and pop
between our body parts,

an encounter with a stag do
that means one of us must sit
on the groom's shoulders,
roast chicken and gravy for dinner,
clubbing, karaoke and do you know
so-and-so. I text you pictures
from Carlingford and spend

all of my minutes unknowingly
until finally the bus drops me
in a carpark in Newcastle at two am
and there you are, your face
rumpled with gorgeous sleep,
my lantern and my tether
to these warding women.

Before we sneak into the house
and hold each other in your single bed,
we linger in the back garden
and glimpse a flash of green
high above the Mournes, a meteor
breaking up above our heads,
the only blessing we seek.

Window

Showering together in our windowless bathroom,
we miss the sunrise, the cries from the nursery
next-door as parents leave, the school traffic,
the work traffic, the dog-walkers, the buses,
the laughter from the nursery, the sunset,
the lights in our front garden flickering on.

We miss it all. I open the folding door,
step out onto the tiles, wipe the walls
and watch you rinse one more time.
You wipe the glass and make a window.

I hand you a towel and sit on the toilet.
You kneel to dry the hair on my legs,
measuring the seasons and I touch the hair
on the back of your neck, measuring days.

Charm for Catching a Train

I buy a return and say she wants the same.
The man gives her an accidental discount,
a kind of love, and she fumbles with the coins.
Without touching, I show her what she needs
and the exact change passes between our palms.
I take her by the elbow and through the gates
before we trade to-go cups to stir and wonder
how the vanilla is more aftertaste than taste.

This also might be love. At the end of the line,
we will find the castle and boats setting sail.
She asks how to alight, whether people
go one at a time or everyone alights together.
The platform number is days spent in love.
A train arrives from the right direction.

ACT THREE

My Actions are Their Dreams

[Enter BRIDGET CLEARY]

I was as thin as a wisp
or I rode a white horse.

I held dances in my house
or I was bedridden for years.

I had an affair with the egg-man
or the neighbour or both.

I had a miscarriage
or I had pneumonia.

I was away with the fairies
or my mother was.

I was buried in a glen,
in a ditch or in a boreen,

in a swamp overgrown with briars
or under the sally trees.

Custody

Clonmel Summer 1895

No. 2 & 3

Regina
v
Michael Cleary
Patrick Boland
John Dunne
Patk Kennedy
James Kennedy
Michael Kennedy
William Kennedy
William Ahern
Mary Kennedy

Murder

Arsonist

I'm a good girl. Why? I mean, hi.
  I just fell in with the misfit crowd.
This town is too small. I lurk in thrift-shops
  and mausoleums until the dust makes me cry.
The echo of my mother's voice is too much
  and I wear sunglasses even in the sewers.
With a splash of moon water, I'm out the window—
  I sneak into the club and snooker your heart.
Maybe I'm an arsonist or maybe I'm a brunette.
  There is always someone to protect.
I want to finish this lollipop in peace.
  I want to make some friends and adopt a cat.

My partner straps a heart monitor to his chest, kisses my cheek and disappears down the Waterford Greenway. I wonder if he is running from Bridget or me. I mosey along the path and cyclists pass me. I hear snatches of their conversations: a garden party, the cost of rent, kids busy with sports and school. E is wearing blue, and he has already disappeared between the sea and the horizon. On a sliver of beach, I look for shells until he returns. When he does, he is topless and glowing in the midday sun. We walk to our car, discussing the weather and what we will cook for dinner. We pass by an older couple, walking slowly in the opposite direction. The woman smiles at us. *Is the Greenway good for running?* she asks. *It is,* E says, *and I'm glad to see European money put to good use.* The woman's husband grunts, then coughs, holding onto her arm. The woman explains that they just got back from England where they were unable to use their sterling fifty-pound notes. She laughs, describing the inconvenience of carrying three thousand pounds in fifties in her handbag for the duration of their month-long holiday. E and I nod as if that amount isn't most of our savings. Later, I calculate that Bridget's life-savings of twenty pounds, which she hid in a coffee can under her bed, would be almost three thousand pounds today. The coffee can vanished after her death.

Touchy-Feely

A dozen roses and a virus make me oogy.
    Can I get this hospital gown in a jewel tone?
A little applesauce will fix me right up.
    I've got eternal dibs on the graveyard shift
and like a swarm of bees I'm beyond overscheduled.
    I need some me-time to polish my teeth.
You know your way around my fish tank heart
    and nothing says love like changing the locks.
Don't tempt me with your touchy-feely talk—
    I want to watch the moonflowers bloom.

Daintily

[Enter KATIE BURKE, Bridget's cousin's daughter, who is a girl of eleven]

Some days at school
girls hiss
and some days they tease
out the truth—
the men said
eat three bites
or down she would go
and daintily she fed.
At midday
when I unwrap
my bread and jam
the lady rises again—
he stripped her,
grabbed a stick
and put his knee
against her chest.
We learn our letters
and I spell her.
My hand crawls
across the page
like a tethered bird
seeking sky.

The After-Party

After all of this is over
    and the future is resolved
I want to throw a party
    for the friends who believed me.
We will have chips and dip
    and unbroken plates.
I will be the lamb
    playing in the nettles
or the ghost of a girl
    wearing knee-high boots
without consequences
    and with nowhere to be.

With Parted Eye

[Enter MINNIE SIMPSON, Bridget's neighbour, who is ten years older than her husband]

All who were outside should stay outside.
The men crowded into her bedroom.
All who were inside should stay inside.

They mixed water, wine and piss.
They took turns dousing her.
All she was outside should stay outside.

The men filed out of the bedroom.
The women formed a circle around her.
All she was inside should stay inside.

I gave her a clean dress.
I washed her soiled clothes.
All I am outside should stay outside.

She knew each of us by sight.
Were my daughters safe and well?
All I am inside should stay inside.

Perhaps we see things with parted eye.
Woman, changeling, person, man.
All we are outside should stay outside.
All we are inside should stay inside.

One hundred years ago, Clonmel was the big town where Bridget trained as a seamstress. Its streets were lit by gas lamps and it was home to not one, but two newspapers. My partner and I are happy to see a familiar coffee shop. We drink lattes and sit in the sun. Someone recognises E; they used to run together. They chat about the latest shoes and next year's races. I sip my drink and write in my notebook. Afterwards, we take a detour to St. Patrick's Well, an ancient site in a leafy sheltered glen. I have only ever read about such wells and how they are aqueous portals to other worlds. I imagine Bridget making Sunday pilgrimages here, like us, to see the medieval cross. Perhaps she would have known the specific prayers and rituals needed to access the well's power. A man with white hair and bright blue eyes circumambulates the well. He is handsomely dressed in a green jacket, blue corduroy trousers and leather shoes. He smiles at us and some of his teeth are missing. Together we listen to the bubbles coming through the limestone. E says he used to visit Struell Wells near Downpatrick in County Down. He once washed his face with holy water to try to clear his skin. The man pats him on the back. I am the only one who is startled by E's familiarity with holy wells. I ask the man if he knows anything about Bridget Cleary. *Several psychics have felt her presence at the well,* he says. *Was she here once or is she here now?* I ask. *She was ahead of her time,* he replies. We introduce ourselves, but he does not offer us his name, only that he used to work in a beef factory. He says he might know some distant relatives of Bridget's, and he will talk to them on my behalf. I thank him and explain we are driving back to Belfast after this. *Is there any way to get in touch with you?* I ask. *I come to the well every day,* he says. The man procures a plastic bottle from somewhere. He fills it with water and pours it out three times before filling it again and offering it to us. We accept the gift and thank the Guardian of the Well.

Pruning

I'm a bad-to-the-bone girl
    or I'm ripe with muscle.
I have tenderly learned
    how to manage my grief—
give me a tampon,
    a yo-yo, a stake
and my best pair
    of pruning shears.
Free therapy for everyone
    who saw the body!
I would rather eat eclairs
    in private with you.
How are you?
    PTSD. I mean, peachy!

Speak Again

[Enter JOHANNA BURKE, Bridget's cousin, who is in the workhouse]

O lady, speak again!
I walk in circles,
pushing the wheel
and grinding corn
into rough flour,
while beyond the walls
my children scatter
like dandelion seeds,
becoming servants
in strange households.
My husband has deserted us
and I walk in circles,
pushing the wheel.
O lady, speak again.

Help

At the turn of the century
    I was wearing leopard print,
kickboxing in the library
    and eating grapes from the vine.
Existing leads to bloodstains,
    frizzy hair and hysteria.
I need a cup of dreamy tea
    and help with my feelings.
The nurse is waving to me
    from the other side of fantasy.
I'm a vortex of joy and I'm quick
    to stab with a meat fork.

Into the Sea

[Enter MICHAEL CLEARY, who sails for Montreal in 1910]

For six and a half years no family
could live more lovingly together.
I attended to the wants of my wife
both day and night when she was ill.
I was the victim of the superstition
of sorcery and under the spell,
I joined my relations in the crime.
I cannot listen to the story any longer.
She's gone and I cast my nets into the sea.

Back in Belfast, we unlock the door and kick off our shoes. My partner begins unpacking immediately, sorting our clothes. He wants to do laundry and get ready for the coming week. Tomorrow, I will continue proofreading other people's manuscripts. I wander around our flat, touching the bed, the fireplace, the pot plants, until everything feels familiar again. I switch on the plugs, preheat the oven and boil the kettle. We both text our parents to let them know we're home. I make E a lemon and ginger tea as a thank you for driving more than six hundred miles. *What did you think of County Tipperary?* I ask. *What did you think of Bridget's world?* he asks. We eat pepperoni pizza and read the news headlines we missed over the weekend. The world is still reassuringly uncertain. My mother texts me: *Did you get what you needed? Or what you wanted?* I want to remind her that Bridget's voice will always be an absence. I promise to call her tomorrow and tell her about the road-trip. E and I are too afraid to drink the water given to us by The Guardian of the Well. Using it to wash dishes seems irreverent. Pouring it down the drain would be wasteful. A spurned blessing could become a curse, neither of which I believe in, so why take our chances. In the shower, we wash ourselves with holy water.

Before the Music Drops

The girls' locker room is a labyrinth,
    a mess of flooded hearts and brains.
I need to get changed for gym class.
    This body is mine until it's not.
I was up late listening to the radio,
    the forecasts of muses and market crashes.
Of course I feel deliciously human
    surrounded by so much yellow tape.
I will be free tonight for a moment
    to think before the music drops.
It's been lovely talking to you.
    It's been so lovely fighting with you.

The Actress

[Enter the actress as herself. There is no proof,
only how she hangs her hat in the bedroom,
how she touches the table, the chairs
and the clock that is ticking merrily.
She sits at the sewing machine unravelling.
Enter me as the ghost and the understudy.
I plunge a hot poker into the butter churn
and all the changelings turn into women
and all the women turn into milk.]

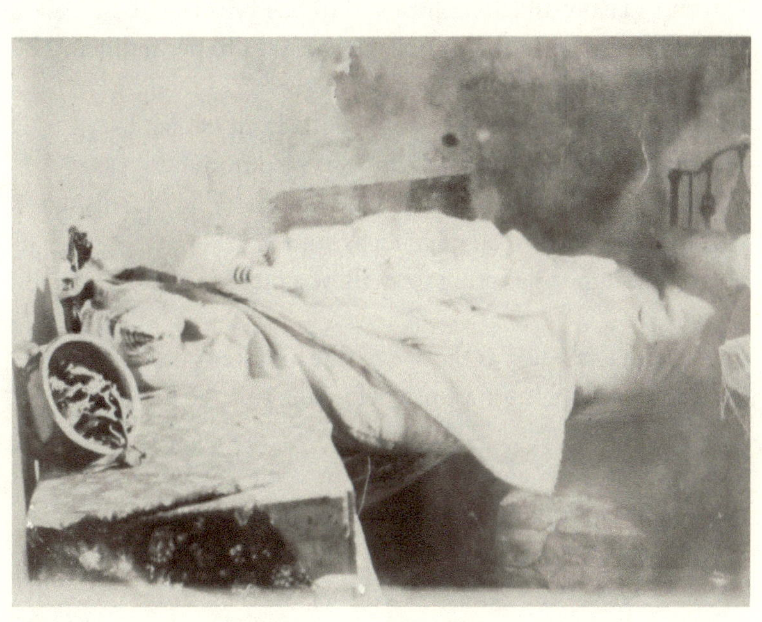

Exit Stage Door

BRIDGET CLEARY sold liquor without a certificate.
She was charged with a fine or six weeks in prison.

BRIDGET CLEARY watched as her house was stoned by men.
The windows were smashed and the door was broken in.

BRIDGET CLEARY asked her husband to buy bread.
He told her to go to the streets and she went to her mother.

BRIDGET CLEARY shooed a relative's cows from her land.
He leapt on her, choking her until she bled from both ears.

BRIDGET CLEARY died alone in an asylum.
She suffocated while trying to swallow a piece of meat.

BRIDGET CLEARY died at the age of one hundred and eleven.
I search newspapers for a story before the story of her death.

I want to burn the archives and begin again.
A woman steps out of the theatre and into the night.

The Engine of My Thoughts

[Re-enter BRIDGET CLEARY]

Humour altered, my father trumpets above my bed,
waking me to restore my former light.

Turn off the light, I say, and my husband outs the light.
A metal spoon or a wooden stump,

a saucepan with yesterday's scrapings,
a candle held aloft and a clean hearth.

I call for sweet water but as he begins it,
he finishes it. My dress alights

and smoke seeps from under my costume.
My other loved ones stir in the guest room

and knock on the door, lovingly locked.
I have some washing if I had the hands.

If I had the hands, I would rather be dancing.
Then I am for the air.

                                        I return
to the corner of the moon

                                                distilled by sleights
where no name fits my nature but my own.

Notes

The epigraphs are attributed to Justice William O'Brien who was the judge for the trial of Bridget Cleary's family and members of her community. They were charged with her murder. The first epigraph appears in 'The Case of Witchcraft in Tipperary' in *The Irish Times* on 5 July 1895. Here O'Brien refers to a passage from *Macbeth* when he says, 'Pleading like angels, trumpet-tongued/ Against the deep damnation of [her] taking off.' O'Brien changes the pronoun in the original lines in order to refer to Bridget Cleary; however, he later insists that 'we are not here acting a play'. The second epigraph appears in 'The Tipperary Witchcraft Case' in *The Irish Times* on 6 July 1895.

The images reproduced in this book are: a bureaucratic report detailing Bridget Cleary's murder (National Archives, NAI/CSO/RP/1895/6694) on p. 15; a photograph of the house where Bridget lived with her family (National Archives, NAI/CBS/1895/9617/S_0002) on p. 42; a list of people put on trial for her murder (National Archives, NAI/CP/Crown Files at Assizes Tipperary/1895) on p. 66; and a photograph of Bridget's bedroom (National Archives, NAI/CBS/1895/9617/S/0002) on p. 81. All images reproduced by kind permission of the Director of the National Archives of Ireland.

Some of the poems in this manuscript incorporate titles, lines and images from several of Shakespeare's plays: *All's Well That Ends Well, Cymbeline, King Lear, Macbeth, A Midsummer Night's Dream, Othello, Romeo and Juliet, The Tempest, Titus Andronicus* and *The Winter's Tale.*

For research, I relied primarily upon *The Burning of Bridget Cleary* by Angela Bourke, which provided information on Bridget Cleary's life, illness, death and the subsequent trial. I referred to *The Cooper's Wife Is Missing* by Joan Hoff and Marian Yeates as well as *Fairy Wife: The Burning of Bridget Cleary* from Wildfire Films. 'My Actions are Their Dreams' draws from stories about Bridget Cleary that can be found online through Dúchas, a project to digitise the National Folklore Collection. 'Haunting' and 'Into the Sea' draw from Michael Cleary's prison records, including his medical records and many petitions for release, which are available in the National Archives of Ireland.

Several of the poems in Act Three very loosely respond to some episodes in seasons 1–3 of *Buffy the Vampire Slayer:* 'Welcome to the Hellmouth', 'The Harvest', 'Teacher's Pet', 'The Pack', 'Angel', 'I, Robot...You, Jane', 'The Puppet Show', 'When She Was Bad', 'Some Assembly Required', 'School Hard', 'Halloween', 'Lie to Me', 'What's My Line (Part 1)', 'Surprise', 'Passion', 'Killed by Death', 'I Only Have Eyes for You', 'Go Fish' and 'Band Candy'. The phrase 'Why? I mean, hi' is a direct quotation from 'Welcome to the Hellmouth'.

These materials were used following the Center for Media & Social Impact's Code of Best Practices in Fair Use for Poetry.

Acknowledgements

Thanks to the editors of the following anthologies and magazines in which earlier versions of some of these poems first appeared: *Abridged, Ambit, Banshee: A Literary Journal, Blackbox Manifold, Enlightenment Legacies* (Ireland in Search of the Legacies of Enlightenment), *Hold Open the Door* (the Ireland Chair of Poetry Commemorative Anthology 2020), *The Honest Ulsterman, The Irish Independent, Magma Poetry* online, *The North, Poetry Birmingham Literary Journal, Poetry Ireland Review, Washing Windows Too* and *Washing Windows III.*

'Stranger' alludes to 'Turn Again' and 'Queen's Gambit' by Ciaran Carson.

Several of the poems in the 'Interval' were first published in my pamphlet, *Charm for Catching a Train* from Green Bottle Press. Thanks to Jennifer Grigg for her ongoing support.

This manuscript was supported by a SIAP award from the Arts Council of Northern Ireland in 2018, the Ireland Chair of Poetry Trust 2021 Project Award and a micro-grant from Neon Books.

Thank you to Pat Boran and Raffaela Tranchino of Dedalus Press for believing in these poems and for making my first book real.

A big thank you to Jessica Traynor for her mentoring via the Irish Writers Centre. An equally big thank you to Moyra Donaldson for her mentoring via the National Mentoring Programme with Words Ireland. To Joe Lines for his advice and support with the early drafts. To Fiona Benson and Ian Duhig for much-needed encouragement and wise, generous readings of the poems. To Martin Doyle at *The Irish Times* for publishing my article 'Bridget Cleary and a poetry journey' online. To Rebecca Tamás for choosing 'Lawful' as the second-place poem in the Ambit Magick poetry competition. To Faber Academy, particularly the anonymous reader who provided detailed manuscript feedback. Thank you to the Society of Authors for facilitating the Hartsop Residency, which provided valuable time to write.

Thank you to some of the artists, musicians and writers who have preserved and reimagined Bridget Cleary's story: Ian Duhig, Tom

Mac Intyre, Medbh McGuckian, Yvonne McGuinness, Margaret Perry, Maija Sofia and Helena Tobin.

Thank you to everyone at the Seamus Heaney Centre at Queen's University Belfast, in particular Stephen Sexton, Fran Brearton, Gail McConnell, Leontia Flynn, Glenn Patterson and Rachel Brown. Being the 2023 Ciaran Carson Writing and the City Fellow provided vital support for this project. Thank you, Ciaran Carson, who welcomed me to Belfast and into Irish poetry. To everyone in Ciaran's Friday workshop where I first shared a few of these poems in 2017–2019. To everyone in the Lemon Experiment for keeping me going. To David Torrans and Claudia Edelmann for No Alibis Bookstore. To Mimi Drew, my high school creative writing teacher. To Shane McCrae, my undergraduate poetry professor at Oberlin College. Thank you, Wendy Beth Hyman, who taught me about Shakespeare's works and worlds at Oberlin College. Her wisdom is integral to this book.

Thank you to the Totten and McPhilemy families. Thank you, Bronagh, for teaching me about wildflowers, Struell Wells and the Historic Environment Map Viewer (https://maps.archaeology.ie/HistoricEnvironment/). Thank you to my friends on both sides of the Atlantic. To Ciara, for her kindness. To Jake, for his wisdom. To Jenna, Tory and Maria for supporting and challenging me. To Bebe, who made our wee house a home. To Marina, for being my oldest friend and braving Belfast rain. Thank you, Alyssa, for long walks in the Crum Woods and even longer letters. Thank you, Caden and Telory, for sisterly wisdom. Thank you, Sophie, for further insight into Shakespeare's plays and being an incredible sister (in-law) for over half my life. Thank you, Marc, for always making me laugh and knowing me inside-out. Thank you, Mom and Dad, for loving me and believing in my poetry. I couldn't have done any of this without you.

Thank you, Eoghan, my loving person. It's a long way to Tipperary (and back). Thank you for making the journey with me. Thank you for reading these poems (again and again and again). You generously offered brilliant insights and edits. I'm a better poet and a happier person with you in my life. Guess what?

www.ingramcontent.com/pod-product-compliance
Lightning Source LLC
LaVergne TN
LVHW091635100826
845152LV00002B/35

* 9 7 8 1 9 1 5 6 2 9 1 6 6 *